Grasping Your Success:
Six Steps to Starting and Legitimizing Your Business

The keys to building a solid foundation for your business to grow!

Michelle P. Jones

Grasping Your Success:
Six Steps to Starting and Legitimizing Your Business

ISBN: 78-1-5323-5343-7

Published In: Indianapolis, Indiana, United State of America

Cover Design: Michelle P. Jones

Edited by: Francine Bond

TABLE OF CONTENTS

FORWARD

Boom! Collision and chaos!

Imagine for a moment that you are cruising along on a quiet road. You have no worries because you are an expert driver with exceptional skills and training. As you drive along the smooth road, with freedom, peace and happiness, you mentally plan out your future and you next move. With excitement, you think about the endless possibilities and the great success life has to offer...BOOM! Out of nowhere a sudden roadblock appears. WHAT WENT WRONG?!?!?! You've followed all the rules, YOU are the expert at what you do, what went wrong? BOOM! BOOM!! BOOM!!!!! More roadblocks, collisions and complete total chaos. You scream HELP!!!

Life has a way of dishing out roadblocks and collisions at the most inopportune times; whether in business, relationships, health or just life in general. These roadblocks and collisions leave us in total chaotic situations, begging us to seek additional help.

I am a business professional with tons of education, skills and experience. I've owned several businesses and have many successes as well as failures to attest to. If anyone thought they had it all together and didn't need help, it would have been me. I had the pleasure of meeting the author, Michelle Jones, at a time when my life was at its most chaotic point. Without hesitation, Michelle offered me great advice, coaching and mentoring that equipped me with the motivation and tools I needed to avoid some of those collisions. I began to use her teachings to remove some road blocks and clear up the most life altering, unsuccessful and chaotic experiences in my life. This allowed me to legitimize my success and be better prepared for the unknown. Michelle has great talent and insight. She is an exceptional life coach with a wealth of knowledge in many areas. Michelle has written many blogs to help others in different aspects of business and life.

If you are in business, plan to be in business or would like to travel the road to establishing and/or keeping a legitimate and successful business; this book would be a powerful and meaningful tool to add to and keep in your toolbox. In the chapters, from beginning to end, Michelle elaborates on important key steps to starting and legitimizing your success. Don't hit those roadblocks head on, avoid unnecessary collisions and don't get buried under mounds of chaos. Add this book to your library and read it cover to cover, as many times as necessary. You too may gain additional knowledge to help build your success. Share the news by encouraging your friends, family and colleagues to invest in this powerful tool.

Tanya Scanlan, MBA

INTRODUCTION

Let's get personal here! You've made the conscious decision to start and grow your business. You may have even decided you want to and make it your main stream of income. You want to leave corporate American and branch out on your own! So, what does that look like? Where do I begin? How do I start my business on a strong foundation that encourages growth? How do I make my passion into a business? How do I start a business when I have no idea what I am doing or where to start? Simply put, you start at the beginning! You start with an idea, passion, ability, skill and/or product, and you expand that into a viable business that will meet peoples' need. Ten (10) years ago, it was much more difficult to start a business. Why? Because of supply and demand! Supply and demand is the amount of a commodity, product or service available and the desire of buyers to purchase it for a price. Think about the product or service you are offering, is there a market for it? Is your passion and/or skill something that people have placed a value on? Have you discovered a simpler or more cost effective way to produce a product or provide a service?

Many people have great business ideas but they failed to either start the business or to start it correctly. For those that have already started your business but didn't do it legally or legitimately, this book is for you as well. You can always start *now* to legitimize your business to ensure it has a solid foundation on which to grow. It's not too late to fix the foundation issues you are experiencing with your business. Just follow the six (6) steps to success in this book and you will begin to see a return on your investment that you never thought possible. I shared with a client recently that once the universe sees that you are being a good steward with the business and its income, it will allow more to come to you. Give yourself and your business the opportunity to exceed everyone's expectations.

As you go on this journey to successful business ownership, I challenge you to do it the right way. Follow these six (6) simple yet life changing steps for both you and your potential business venture. Starting your business is one of the most important things you will ever do. As you begin to learn what it takes it will all seem a little overwhelming when you first start off, but it isn't. By following these six (6) simple steps, you will have everything you need to start and legitimize your business. Trust me when I say this will be the experience of a lifetime.

STEP ONE:

REGISTERING YOUR BUSINESS

Step One: Registering Your Business

The first thing you MUST do when deciding to start and legitimize your business is to register your business with your State's Secretary of State's (SOS) office. I live in the state of Indiana and I will be using the process for starting a business in Indiana as the basis for the examples used in this book. Each state has a similar process but the steps suggested are the same no matter what state you are in. Registering with the SOS in your state is a **key** step, as you cannot have two (2) businesses within the same state with the same name. The SOS office will be able to tell you if the name you are wanting to call your business is an existing business or not. If it is and you have already been doing business under that name, no worries. Create a Parent Company that is doing business as (d/b/a) the name that has already been registered. That way you will be able to continue using your original name for business purposes. The following are the suggested steps for registering your business:

Register the business with your Domicile (Home) state Secretary of State's Office

Register the business with your domicile (home) state Secretary of State Office to ensure that your business name is viable and there isn't another business already in existence with that name. Once registered, you will receive an "Articles of Organization" form/letter provided by the SOS which is needed to open a bank account and/or obtain credit in the business name. The process is quite easy.

Go to the business' home state's SOS website (for Indiana it's www.in.gov/sos). Select "Business Services Division," "Form a New Business" then follow the instructions as given on the website. When you have successfully answered the questions and paid the required fee, your company will be registered with your domicile state Secretary of State's office.

Things you need to know and have prior to completing the process:

Business name: The online system will take you through the process of checking if the name you have selected for your business is already in existence. During the process, you will need to have the start or effective date of your business or your parent company.

Setting up business as a Parent Company: If the above process reveals that another company is already doing business under the name you've selected, create a Parent Company that is doing business as (d/b/a) your business' name. That way you will be able to continue using your original business name with a d/b/a (Doing Business As) distinction (i.e. Delicious Delights by Daphne is the name of the business already in existence, when registering the business with the SOS use a different name "Triple D's Delights d/b/a Delicious Delights by Daphne"). This allows you to register the Parent Company with your domicile state SOS office. By doing this you are conducting business under the name that people are familiar with and/or recognizes as you take your business to the next level.

Business address for the business: The online application will ask for the "Principal Office Address" which cannot be a P.O. Box. If you need to use an address, other than the physical location of the business, go to the UPS or FEDEX store and rent a box. They will provide you with a physical address and unit number that will be accepted by your domicile state SOS office and the IRS. It will also be the place where you will receive mail for the business.

Registered Agent's Information: You will be asked if your business' Registered Agent is an individual or a business. In most cases this will be an 'individual' unless you have a business that you have already registered with the SOS office and the "new" business you are creating is a subsidiary. In other words, the new business can be registered under a company that you have already registered with the SOS. If that is the case, select 'business.' Most of us will use "individual" as the Registered Agent for our business.

Principal's Information for the business: Know your business distinction (This will be discussed in greater detail under Registering with the IRS section of the book.). The questions asked here will force you to list your business distinction/entity. There are different ones: LLC, S-Corporation, Corporation, Sole Proprietor, etc.) For example, if you have selected LLC as your business' distinction, you will be asked if the LLC will be managed by managers or if it is a Single Member LLC (A Single Member LLC is viewed in the same way as a sole proprietor business. Both scenarios are expected to reflect the business' activities on their individual/personal federal tax return), and you will want to select "yes" the LLC will be managed by managers (if you want to keep your finances and the business' finances separate), and complete the Principle Information section with your information as the owner of the business. At the end of the application, it will ask you to sign and provide your title. In most cases, you will select 'manager' to identify you as the managing member.

Attachments Section: Unless you have, additional articles/information significant to the business leave this area blank. The Secretary of State's office will provide you with your

"Articles of Incorporation" that you will need to keep handy in your important business records' file.

Payment: The SOS office will require you to pay a fee to register your business with their office. Depending upon whether you are registering your business as a "for profit" or a "non-profit" business will determine the fee you will be charged. If you are registering as a nonprofit organization, you will be charged a minimum of $25 (depending upon the state you are in) or if you are registering as a for profit business you will be charged a minimum of $75 (depending upon the state you are in). You can pay the fee online or take your payment into your domicile state SOS office and pay it in person. Once the payment is submitted, you will receive your "Articles of Incorporation" paperwork either in person, via email or U.S. Mail. The delivery of your "Articles of Incorporation" is dependent upon how you submitted payment and how you requested it to be sent.

Register with the IRS to get your Employer Identification Number (EIN)

Your social security number (SSN) shouldn't be your business identifier. By using your social security number, you leave yourself and ***ALL*** your personal assets unprotected and liable if there is a suit against the business or if the business fails and a court orders you to pay off existing debt/liabilities.

The Employer Identification Number (EIN) is the best legal identifying number for your business. It will also be used when identifying your business with the Federal Internal Revenue Service and the domicile state Internal Revenue Service. The process is quite easy.

Completing the Application: Go to www.irs.gov and under "Tools" click on "Apply for an EIN." Follow the instructions and once you have successfully answered the questions you will be given an Employer Identification Number (EIN). There are other ways to apply for and register for an EIN (i.e. online, by fax, by mail and/or by telephone); however, the online process is the easiest and quickest method.

Things you need to know or have to apply for an EIN:

SSN of the principal officer, general partner, grantor, owner, trustor, etc.

Name and address for the business: The name of the business provided on this online application ***MUST*** be the same name as registered with your State's SOS office. Also, the address used on the online application ***MUST*** be the same address used when registering your business with the SOS office. It ***CANNOT*** be a P.O. Box.

Registering a Parent Company: If you registered your business with your State's SOS office using the Parent Company scenario, be sure and use the same name to register for the EIN. You have already done the work. Remember you want to work smarter not harder.

Know your businesses distinction: When applying for an EIN it will ask you what is your business entity (i.e. LLC, Inc., Non-Profit, etc.).

A ***Sole Proprietorship*** is the simplest form of a business organization. Proprietorships have no existence apart from the owners. The liabilities associated with the business are the personal liabilities of the owner, and the business terminates upon the proprietor's death. The proprietor undertakes the risks of the business to the extent of risking his/her personal assets. A sole proprietorship is the easiest and least expensive business entity to establish; and the business can be terminated at the will of the owner.

A ***Limited Liability Corporation (LLC)*** is a business entity allowed by state statute that's formed by registering the business with the domicile state SOS office. The owners or members are protected from some or all liability for acts and debts of the LLC, depending on domicile state's shield laws, and do not need to be organized for profit. An LLC offers its Members operational flexibility and income benefits with limited liability exposure; and in many states, an LLC may have only one member who may have the benefits of a sole proprietorship but it limits their liability. There can be ***only*** one (1) active LLC within a state at a time (two (2) LLCs with the same name cannot be registered in the same state within the continental United States).

A ***Corporation (Inc.)*** is a legal entity, operating under state law, with restrictions by its charter. Its charter grants it certain legal powers, rights, privileges and liabilities, and can be established by a person or group of people with a charter from the domicile Secretary of State office with their articles of incorporation on file. A Corporation is double taxed. It is first taxed on its profits and secondly, is taxed on the distributed stockholder dividends (as capital gains). The owner's personal assets cannot be seized by creditors and it has a perpetual life span that's subject to the domicile state's laws and regulations.

A ***Small Business Corporation*** or ***S-Corporation*** is a special closed corporation created to provide small corporations with a tax advantage, if IRS Code requirements are met. It allows a person or group of people to establish a legal entity by filing articles of incorporation with the domicile state SOS office granting it certain legal powers, rights, privileges and liabilities. Corporate taxes are waived and reported by the owners on their individual federal income tax returns, avoiding the "double taxation" of regular corporations. To become a S-Corporation the owner must elect this status by using Form 2553 (Election by a Small Business Corporation) with the IRS within two months and 15 days of the beginning of the tax year the election is to take effect, or at any time during the tax year preceding the tax year it is to take effect (see https://www.irs.gov/pub/irs-pdf/i2553.pdf for more information).

A ***Non-Profit Organization (Inc.)*** is an organization that has been formed by a group of people in order "to pursue a common not-for-profit goal" and/or to pursue a stated goal without the intention of distributing excess revenue to members or leaders. A nonprofit organization is often dedicated to furthering a specific social cause or advocating for a point of view. Nonprofits may apply for tax exempt status, so that the organization itself may be exempt from income tax and other taxes. A nonprofit organization uses its surplus revenues to further achieve its purpose or mission. Non-profit organizations includes: public charities, private foundations, educational organizations, employee associations, veteran's organizations, business leagues, state-chartered credit unions, child care organizations and teachers' retirement fund associations, etc.

EIN Certification Letter: Once the application process is completed, you will receive a letter via email, fax or U.S. mail identifying your EIN number and certifying your business as being a registered business with the federal government. Keep that letter in a safe place and on hand. Treat it in the same manner you would your SSN. There may be times when creditors will request a copy of the letter or you may need to it for business purposes.

REGISTER WITH YOUR STATE'S DEPARTMENT OF REVENUE (DOR) AND THE IRS.

It is important for you to register your business with your home State's Department of Revenue (DOR) and the IRS. This is necessary for tax purposes (i.e. property tax, sales tax, employment tax, and/or federal income taxes). If you sell retail products, you will need to obtain a sales tax permit/number to ensure that all taxes collected are paid to the State where business is being conducted. If you hire employees and/or purchase property under the business' name, you need to understand your business' obligations where property, income and/or employment taxes are concerned. This information will be disseminated to you by the revenue agencies listed above. They also have people available who can answer any questions regarding the process of registering your business with them and/or being assigned a sales tax permit/number. By not doing so, you jeopardize your business and may be faced with prison, penalties, and/or fines for not paying the required taxes from products sold, taxes collected from employees and/or for failure to pay business/corporate taxes annually.

APPLY FOR A DUNS NUMBER

If you plan on bidding on state, local or federal contracts, you will need a DUNS number. The D&B D-U-N-S® Number is a unique nine-digit identifier for businesses. It is used to establish a Dun & Bradstreet business credit file, which is often referenced by lenders and potential business partners to help predict the reliability and/or financial stability of the company in question. If you want to bid on government proposals, you will need to get a D-U-N-S Number for each physical location of your business. To register for a DUNS number, you will need the following information:

1. Your Legal Name
2. Legal Name of the Business (Headquarters) and address for your business
3. Identify if you are 'Doing Business As' (DBA) or the other name by which your business is commonly recognized
4. Physical address, city, state and zip code (if different from headquarters address)
5. Mailing Address (if different from headquarter/physical address)
6. Telephone number
7. Contact name and title
8. Number of employees at your physical location
9. Identify whether you are a Home-Based Business

You can apply for a free DUNS number and receive it in approximately thirty (30) days or you can get your DUNS number expedited in five (5) business days or less with a DUNSFile™ (The DUNs number is used to create your business credit file or a DUNSFile™. The process for creating a DUNSFile™ is provided on the Dun and Bradstreet website (www.dandb.com/duns-file/). This is the number that will house your business' credit worthiness and business. This is an important step, if you plan on bidding on state, local and/or federal contract/proposals.

CERTIFY YOUR BUSINESS AS A MBE/WBE/VBE (IF APPLICABLE)

Each city, state and the federal government has a department that certifies Minority-Owned Business Enterprises (MBE), Women-Owned Business Enterprises (WBE) and Veteran-Owned Business Enterprises (VBE). In Indiana, the Minority and Women's Business Enterprises Division actively promotes, monitors and enforces the standards for certification of minority, women and veteran business enterprises for the state. To qualify for either of the previously stated distinctions, a firm/business ***MUST*** be 51 percent owned by qualifying minorities, women or veterans who possess expertise in the field, who control the business enterprise and who are US citizens. This process can be tedious, I suggest that you contact the city, state and/or federal department that handles the certification process. Each office has monthly meetings to discuss the certification process, answer any questions and discuss what's needed during the certification process. You never know it may be a door you never thought was available to you. It doesn't hurt to check it out!

•

STEP TWO:

CERTIFICATIONS, TRAINING & LICENSING

STEP TWO: CERTIFICATIONS, TRAININGS AND LICENSING

Certifications, Trainings and Licensing are based upon the Industry in which you have chosen to conduct business. Many of the industries in which we choose to do business are regulated, however, there are some that aren't regulated. If the Industry in which you have chosen to do business is not regulated, make sure you look for a ***mentor***. Every Industry is going to be different, and will require different trainings, certifications and/or licensing procedures. Make sure you know what they are to ensure you run a successful and viable business. A ***mentor*** can help make sure you have pertinent Industry information and will help you avoid some of the known pitfalls within your chosen industry.

Find a Mentor: Your mentor can be someone you trust, can work with and/or learn from, and who has at least five (5) years of experience successfully running a like company within the same industry. I know I have suggested that you have a mentor if you are working within an unregulated Industry, I also suggests that you have a mentor in a regulated Industry as well. A mentor is an invaluable resource for someone just starting out in business.

A mentor can help you navigate through setting up your company and running your business. A mentor can inform you of the tricks of the trade, expectations, certifications, licenses, trainings and other necessary information to ensure that you conduct business per the Industry's standards.

Create Business Contacts/Relationships: Build professional contacts/relationships with people you meet while setting up and conducting business. You never know, your business relationship with them may bring you additional business opportunities and/or provide you access to other business owners that were previously out of your reach. You never know who knows who in business.

Know the Industry: Do your research and learn as much as possible about your chosen Industry. Know the specific regulations within your Industry specifically within the home state of your business. Each state may require something different. They may also accept the certifications/licenses from another state in lieu of you going through their certification/licensing process. Remember knowledge is power and when you know better you can do better!

Renewal Process for your License(s): Each state has a department responsible for issuing licenses, certifications or registrations. In Indiana, the Indiana Department of Insurance issues licenses, certifications or registrations for all Industries. Make sure you keep up with the date that your license expires and the renewal process. Some licenses require you to take a specific number of continuing education (CE) credit hours to renew. This number will vary depending upon the license, the state and/or industry. When the license was originally issued, you were notified of the required CE credit hours necessary to renew. Adhere to the information provided, and if you don't remember, refer to the licensing agency. CE classes are necessary because Industry standards change and the climate in which you do business changes also! The CE will keep you updated on any changes that have occurred since you originally received your license or since your last renewal. Make sure you keep up with your license renewal date! By doing so it will allow you to continue conducting business, keep you from having to pay fines, additional fees or jump through unnecessary hoops to get your license reinstated.

Remember, you are starting and legitimizing your business, by obtaining the necessary certifications, licenses and/or trainings you are ensuring your business is set to be a premier business within your chosen Industry. If you start off right, you have a better opportunity to have a successful, highly respectable and viable business.

STEP THREE:

ONLINE PRESENCE

STEP THREE: ON-LINE PRESENCE

As you are aware, we live in a digital age, and it is imperative that your business has an online presence. There are many different mediums you can use for your online presence such as a website, Facebook page, E-commerce platform and other social media pages. All of them will allow your business to reap major benefits, but without an online presence, you are basically leaving money on the table for someone else to access. It is not necessary for your company to conduct business online; however, it is imperative that it has an online presence so that customers and potential customers can ***see*** you online. If they can't see you online, you could be losing the opportunity to increase your customer base and advertise the products/services your business offers. Here are some of the mediums that businesses currently use as their online presence:

Website: Your business ***NEEDs*** a website. It can be extremely basic; however, it will need to contain your business' basic and fundamental information for easy access by customers and/or potential customers. Your website should clearly identify your products/services and the type of business/industry in which you conduct business. You can create a basic website using a free platforms/services (i.e. WordPress, Wix, Weebly, GoDaddy, Squarespace, Website Builder and Jimdo. Some of these free platforms also offer specialized website building services for a fee.) or you can pay to have a professional website created and maintained for your business. Your website will give your customer base a platform in which to communicate with you, purchase products/services and/or leave testimonials.

Once your website is launched, it is very important that you can be found by search engines. Consider **Search Engine Optimization** (SEO) for your website. The purpose of the SEO is to make it easy for search engines to find your website and list it in their 'organic' (as opposed to 'paid') results. The major search engines include Google, Yahoo and Bing. These search engines connect people all over the world to the content they are looking for, products they want and services they desire. The search engines are the holders of information and you want your website to be amongst the information they provide to connect you with your customers and/or potential customers.

It is important that you continuously engage with your customers and seek out potential customers by **creating a mailing list for your business.** Maintain your online presence by sending out monthly or quarterly newsletters, posting advertisements of upcoming products and/or services and sharing your company's current news.

Social Media: Social media improves your business' chances of generating additional revenue and it helps you build a loyal customer base. Social Media allows customers, potential customers and other interested parties to engage with your business daily. Take the time to consider the various social media sites to see if any will assist you in meeting your business' goals and objectives. There are two (2) social media sites that are utilized most often by businesses: Facebook and Twitter. Both sites allow you to post your business' news, tips, photos, videos, allow customers to write testimonials, etc. There are others so be sure to research ***ALL*** the available social media platforms and determine which will work best for your business (i.e. Instagram, Google+, LinkedIn, YouTube, Pinterest, Tumblr, FourSquare, etc.).

Once you have decided which social media platforms to use, get a clear idea of the content you want to share. Engagement is the key to promoting your brand, services and/or products. Make the content you share is compelling, interesting and engaging to your customers and potential customers. If it is, they will be more likely to share your page with others, which will drive more traffic to your site and hopefully increase your sales.

Once again, having an online presence is paramount to the success of your business. Before people make decisions on what to buy and who to buy it from, they research the companies providing the products/services they need. Make sure your company's website is one of the sites they can find and review when making their buying decision.

STEP FOUR:

BUSINESS INSURANCE

Step Four: Business Insurance

It is imperative that you have Business Insurance to cover you in case of an incident or accident. There are specific insurance products for every Industry. For example, within the medical industry there is malpractice insurance for doctors, errors and omissions insurance for real estate and insurance agents, general liability and other types of insurance depending on your Industry. If you don't know, if you are not sure, if you have not been educated on the correct insurance you need for your business, ***ASK***!! This is another area where your mentor will be an invaluable resource! If you don't have a mentor, call an Insurance Broker and pick their brain. Allow them to correctly inform you of the business insurance required for your Industry and what that insurance package entails.

Make sure you ***know what the Insurance requirements are for your Industry and you know what is covered within your insurance package***! Ask specific and open-ended questions that requires an explanation which could potentially trigger more questions for you to ask. I cannot stress this enough, ***know what the specifications are for the insurance requirements you need for your Industry***. Some Industries are more difficult to insure and local or well-known insurance companies may not provide the type of business insurance you need therefore you may have to find an insurance broker.

If you have rented a space for the purposes of conducting business, make sure your General Liability Insurance covers your property being housed there. This insurance is most likely included in your General Liability Insurance, but don't assume, ask! Knowledge is power!! Information opens doors and brings understanding! The more information you have, the better equipped you are to handle anything that comes up.

Use a reputable Insurance Broker: Make sure you use an Insurance Broker who can connect with other insurance companies and who offers the type of insurance needed for your business. There have been some cases where businesses had business insurance and not the insurance specific to their Industry, and only found out the difference when there was an incident or accident that the insurance company refused to cover due to having the wrong insurance coverage. A broker can secure all the insurance needed for your company even if it requires them to use different insurance companies to secure the best insurance package for your company.

If you have employees or in some cases independent contractors, you ***must*** have a **Workers' Compensation Insurance** for your Company. Most clients contracting with a company will request that your Company provide them with a certificate of insurance showing Workers' Compensation Insurance and other types of insurance requested by the client. Most of the time the proof of coverage is required before they will sign a contract with your Company. The amount of workers' compensation insurance needed and its corresponding premium is based off your Company's expected gross salaries for independent contractors or employees, or the gross revenue paid out in salaries to independent contractors or employees during your Company's previous year of business. Each state has different specifications of what the workers' compensation insurance is going to look like. In most cases, you can obtain Workers' Compensation Insurance from the company that's providing you with your business insurance.

If the insurance company is unable to secure your workers' compensation insurance an Insurance Broker can place you with a **State's Sponsored Workers' Compensation Pool.** Your Broker will complete the application to obtain the State Sponsored Worker's Compensation Insurance. You will be notified if you have been approved and what the specifications are of the approval. The pool allows businesses in specific Industries to acquire the insurance coverages they need.

To do business today, you ***must*** have industry specific business insurance and not just any general business insurance. If you are providing services, the companies you contract with expect you to have the proper business insurance and to show proof of that insurance before they will begin a contractual relationship. Do yourself a favor and ensure you have all your ducks in a row so that you can set your business up for exponential growth.

STEP FIVE:

CONTRACTUAL AGREEMENT - SERVICES CONTRACTS

STEP FIVE: CONTRACTUAL AGREEMENT – SERVICES CONTRACTS

Make sure that your Contracts/Services Agreements are air tight and legally binding documents. It would be a shame to have a wonderfully worded contract that isn't legally binding because one (1) paragraph nullifies your entire contract. One simple paragraph will fix that problem, but by not having it in your contract leaves your Company exposed to unwanted and unnecessary litigation:

"If any provision of this Agreement is held illegal or unenforceable in a judicial proceeding, such provision shall be severed and shall be inoperative, and the remainder of this Agreement shall remain operative and binding for all Parties."

Make sure you have a lawyer or someone who has legalese to assist you in drafting your contracts/service agreements.

There are a lot of **Online Sites that will assist your Company with legal services** such as creating legally binding contracts and documents specific to your Company's structure and Industry's standards (i.e. RocketLawyer.com, LawDepot.com, Onecle.com, Biztree.com, FormSwift.com, etc.). Some of the sites will charge a fee while others will provide the legal services free of change on a one-time basis. Be sure to investigate the site before signing up to ensure it can meet your specific needs and that you can afford their legal services.

There are Non-Profit Legal Organizations and Law firms that provide **Pro Bono Legal Services** to small and medium sized businesses that cannot afford a paid attorney. They will assist the business owner in making sure their company, contracts and/or services agreements are legally sound and binding documents.

If you are unable to find a business or law firm that is willing to assist you as a pro bono client, then contact your local School of Law's Legal Clinics for assistance. During the school year, they have law students who work for their **Non-Profit/For Profit Legal Clinics** that may be able to assist you. They will review your needs, determine if they can assist you and if so, they will assign law students to work on your legal project as their semester project. All legal services are provided pro bono because the students need the experience and the legal clinics prefer using existing businesses as clients to provide their students with invaluable experience.

If your Company provides ten (10) different services to their Clients, then you need to have ten (10) different Services Contracts. One for each area of business or for each service being provided to Clients. When you get business insurance for your company you will be audited by the insuring company. Some of the items requested will be your service contracts, gross sales revenue, employee salary information, etc. The outcome of the audit can affect the amount of business insurance you pay in the future. They can refund for an overpayment or identify additional premiums you will pay because your insurance did not adequately meet the needs of your Company. Make sure you have a back-up plan in place for all company records. **Keep files on-site and off-site with a regularly occurring back-up system** (i.e. home safe, safe deposit box, safe location off-site, on-line Cloud, etc.). This will protect your administrative documents, business documents, employee documents, proprietary information, products and services information, etc. This back-up system protects your information if your files, computers, offices and/or on-site business information is destroyed. This will allow you to protect your proprietary, administrative and business information.

STEP SIX:

SOLIDIFY YOUR HUMAN RESOURCES PROCESS

Step Six: Solidify Your Human Resources Process

A lot of companies today have opted to have independent contractors because independent contractors are responsible for paying their own taxes, their own unemployment payments to the State and provide their own medial insurance. The independent contractor doesn't receive benefits from the company unless it is contractually agreed upon. If you employ independent contractors, your company ***must*** have them sign an independent contractor's agreement prior to their first day work with your company. Other companies hire full time, part time or temporary employees to assist with the everyday running of the business, provide the contracted services to their Clients and/or manufacture the products they sale. Regardless of the type of employee a company decides to use, they still need to make sure they have verifiable and documented pre-employment, employment and post-employment documentation.

When you start your business, and hire either employees or independent contractors, you ***must*** have an **Employment Application** specific to the Industry in which your company conducts business for them to complete. If not, it could leave your company exposed and liable for the unprofessional behaviors and/or conduct of an employee or potential employee. When you are dealing with your employees (or independent contractors), you must make sure you are protecting your proprietary, business, and/or financial information. That includes anything that is specific, significant and/or unique to you doing business within your state and industry!

Non-Compete Agreement or clause basically states that the employee will not go after any contract or undercut any contract that their employer or potential employer has with a Client for a specific time-period after the employee's employment/relationship is terminated with the company. I suggest the time-period be a minimum of seven (7) years after the employee's employment relationship has been terminated or their pre-employment relationship is completed with the company. This provides your company with a legal recourse should the employee/potential employee fail to live up to the signed agreement.

Non-Disclosure Agreement or clause basically states that any proprietary information or any specific information significant and/or unique your business is not to be discussed outside of regular business operations to anyone employed or not employed by the Company. This includes how you do business, how you interact with clients, how you interact with other employees, how you interact with office personnel, etc. This will remain in effect for a specified time-period after the employee's employment is terminated or the pre-employment relationship has ended with the Company. I suggest a time-period of seven (7) years after the employee's separation or the pre-employment relationship has ended with the Company. By including the non-disclosure agreement/clause, you will protect your company's finances, employment practices, proprietary and/or administrative information by informing your employees/potential employees upfront of your expectations of them.

This is suggested as a part of the Application Process because during the pre-employment/hiring process, specifically the interview, proprietary information may be shared with the applicant. By clearly stating your expectations, it deters the applicant from attempting to use the information obtained to start their own business or solicit business from your clients now or in the near future. It gives you a legal recourse should the applicant fail to adhere to the terms of the application. Specifically, those areas that they initialed, and where their signature is affixed to the application signifying their compliance to the terms contained therein.

After completing the application process with a potential employee, you may want to make an **Offer of Employment**. This process will be different depending on whether the person will be hired as a specific type of employee or an independent contractor. Both distinctions will provide you with the necessary workforce to run your business and provide quality and professional products/services to your clients.

An **Offer Letter** is not an employment contract. It is a formal written document sent by a potential employer to a potential employee offering employment. The letter confirms the details of the offer of employment, which can include the job description, salary, benefits, start date, etc. The potential employee should sign the letter as their acceptance of employment and the benefits contained therein.

An **Independent Contractor** is a person that provides goods or services to another entity/business under specified terms in a contract or within a verbal agreement. Unlike an employee, an independent contractor does not work regularly for an employer but works when required. An Independent Contractor Agreement/Contract governs the relationship between a company and an independent contractor. It identifies the terms of the contract both legally and logistically, and makes sure both parties are protected.

How you implement your Human Resources Process isn't as important as having one. Just as your business, insurance needs to be based upon Industry specifics, your Human Resources Process need to be specific to the needs of your business. Don't wait until something happens to put your Human Resources Process in place. If you put a process in place now, you can update it whenever necessary and/or as your business grows. Remember we want to work smarter not harder.

According to "***The Complete Guide to Human Resources for Small Business***," there are three (3) basic things you must implement to cover the bases:

1. **Employee Files**. This is where you keep all specific files for the employees or independent contractors you employ in your business.
2. **Employee Handbook**. Having an employee or independent contractor's handbook is a must. Your handbook serves two (2) very important purposes: letting your employees or general contractors know what you expect of them, and protecting your business in case there is a dispute.

Display Required Posters. Depending on the laws of the country and/or state your business is in, you may be required to post information in an easily accessible place. These vary from place to place, so you will want to work with a local government agency or legal counsel to make sure you have met the requirements. There are also companies that provide packets of posters depending upon your location to help make the process easier.

CONCLUSION

GRASPING YOUR SUCCESS

The previously identified six (6) steps are meant to help you start and legitimize your business. If you follow the six (6) steps contained herein, you can have a viable business built on a solid foundation, which is set to grow exponentially. I suggest that after 2-3 years in business you take another look at your services agreements/contracts, business insurance package and your human resources processes to make sure that it continues to meet your Industry's standards, company's needs and expectations. Industries and standards change with time, and you'll want to make sure that your company's contract/agreements and employment practices meet the current standards. I have given you a lot of information. So now what? What do you do at this point? You conduct your business in a professional and Industry specific manner. Go out and look for clients and begin to operate your business legitimately and purposefully. Know what areas you want to work and then make it happen. Will it be tough just starting out? Yes! Will it be hard legitimizing your business after you've been in business and have developed certain mindsets that aren't meeting Industry standards? Yes! It is stressful and it is time consuming because we want everything now. But keep this in mind, everything is a process! When you work the process, the process will work for you!

Companies are looking for professional and viable businesses that can provide the services/products they need in a timely, professional and efficient manner. Being able to do that is easy when you have the right information, and when your Company is built on a solid foundation. You cannot pull a Certificate of Insurance out of the air and provide it to a potential client if you don't have business insurance. You cannot provide a client/potential client with your EIN if you don't have one. You cannot hold an employee/independent contractor accountable/responsible for competing against you with a client within a seven (7) year period, if you have never made sure that they signed the non-compete agreement and independent contractor's agreement prior to starting work. There's a lot of moving pieces to this but trust me if you follow these six (6) basic steps to starting and legitimizing your business then you'll have what it takes to have a successful business set for exponential growth.

A word of caution to those of you who are legitimizing your business, ***don't half step*** and only complete the steps you think you need. When you begin to legitimize your business, you will also have to have a mind shift. You **must** move from how you ran your business in the past to thinking about your Industry standards and how that plays into you running a viable and successful business in the future.

I have a client that in the past was wasting money by allowing others to fix whatever was wrong in their business. Now, since money is tighter, they have to change how they think, learn how to do things themselves and be financially smart in how they utilize their finances. It has caused them to change how they think about and run their business, and how they manage their finances. Again, it's a process that takes time. So, trust that it will pay off if you work the process as described herein. I believe in you, now I want you to believe in yourself and believe that GREATNESS lies within you! Now go and be GREAT!!!

Bibliography

1. www.in.gov/sos State of Indiana, Secretary of State's Office, May 2017
2. www.irs.gov Internal Revenue Service, Starting a Business, May 2017
3. www.RocketLawyer.com Rocket Lawyer, Legal made simple, May 2017
4. www.dandb.com What is a D&B DUNS Number, June 2017
5. www.in.gov/idoa/mwbe Indiana Department of Administration - Certify your M/WBE Business, May 2017
6. www.wikipedia.org Independent Contractor definition, May 2017

ADDENDUM

LISTING OF SECRETARY OF STATE OFFICE IN THE USA

1. Alabama Secretary of State, http://sos.alabama.gov, (334) 242-5324 (Phone)/ (334) 240-3138 (Fax)
2. Alaska Department of Commerce, Community, and Economic Development, https://www.commerce.alaska.gov/web, (907) 465-2550 (Phone)/ (907) 465-2974 (Fax)
3. Arizona Corporation Commission, http://ecorp.azcc.gov, (602) 542-3026 (Phone)/ (602) 542-4990 (Fax)
4. Arkansas Secretary of State, http://www.sos.arkansas.gov, (888) 233-0325 (Phone)/ (501) 682-3437 (Fax)
5. California Secretary of State, http://www.ss.ca.gov/, 916.657.5448 (Phone)
6. Colorado Secretary of State, Colorado Registered Agent Services, http://www.sos.state.co.us, (303) 894-2200 (Phones)/ (303) 869-4864
7. Connecticut Secretary of State, Connecticut Registered Agent Services, http://www.ct.gov/sots/site/default.asp, (860) 509-6003 (Phone)/ (860) 509-6068 (Fax)
8. Delaware Secretary of State, Delaware Registered Agent Services, http://www.corp.delaware.gov/, (302) 739-3073 (Phone)/ (302) 739-3812 (Fax)
9. District of Columbia, District of Columbia Department of Consumer & Regulatory Affairs, http://www.dcra.dc.gov/, (202) 442-4400 (Phone)/ (202) 442-9445 (Fax)
10. Florida Department of State, http://www.dos.state.fl.us/, (850) 245-6000 (Phone)/ (850) 245-6014 (Fax)
11. Georgia, Office of Secretary of State, http://sos.ga.gov/, (404) 656-2817 (Phone)/ (404) 657-6380 (Fax)

12. Hawaii, Department of Commerce and Consumer Affairs, https://portal.ehawaii.gov/, (808) 586-2744 (Phone)/ (808) 586-2733 (Fax)
13. Idaho, Office of the Secretary of State, http://www.sos.idaho.gov/, (208) 334-2301 (Phones)/ (208) 334-2080 (Fax)
14. Illinois Secretary of State, http://ilsos.com/, (217) 782-6961 (Phone)
15. Indiana Secretary of State, http://www.in.gov/sos/business/index.htm, (317) 232-6576 (Phone)/ (317) 233.3387 (Fax)
16. Iowa, Office of the Secretary of State, http://www.sos.state.ia.us/, (515) 281-5204 (Phone)/ (515) 242-5953 (Fax)
17. Kansas Secretary of State, http://www.kssos.org/, (785) 296-4564 (Phone)/ (785) 296-4570 (Fax)
18. Kentucky Secretary of State, http://sos.ky.gov/Pages/default.aspx, 502.564.3490 (Phone)/ 502.564.5687 (Fax)
19. Louisiana Secretary of State, http://www.sos.la.gov/Pages/default.aspx, (225) 925-4704 (Phone)/ (225) 932-5314 (Fax)
20. Maine State Department, http://www.state.me.us/sos/, (207) 624-7736 (Phone)/ (207) 287-5428 (Fax)
21. Maryland Secretary of State, http://www.sos.state.md.us/, (410) 767-1340 (Phone)/ (410) 333-7097 (Fax)

22. Massachusetts Secretary of State, http://www.sos.state.md.us/, (617) 727-9640 (Phone)/ (617) 742-4538 (Fax)
23. Michigan Department of Labor & Economic Growth, http://www.sec.state.ma.us/, (517) 241-6470 (Phone)/ (517) 241-0538 (Fax)
24. Minnesota Secretary of State, http://www.sos.state.mn.us/, (651) 296-2803 (Phone)/ (651) 297-7067 (Fax)
25. Mississippi Secretary of State, http://www.sos.ms.gov/, (601) 359-1633 (Phone)/ (601) 359-1607 (Fax)
26. Missouri Corporations Division, http://www.sos.mo.gov/, (573) 751-4153 (Phone)/ (573) 751-5841 (Fax)
27. Montana Secretary of State, http://www.sos.mt.gov/, (406) 444-3665 (Phone)/ (406) 444-3976 (Fax)
28. Nebraska Secretary of State, http://www.sos.ne.gov/dyindex.html, (402) 471-4079 (Phone)/ (402) 471-3666 (Fax)
29. Nevada Secretary of State, http://www.nvsos.gov/, (775) 684-5708 (Phone)/ (775) 684-5725 (Fax)
30. New Hampshire Secretary of State, http://sos.nh.gov/, (603) 271-3246 (Phone)/ (603) 271-3247 (Fax)
31. New Jersey, New Jersey Division of Revenue, http://www.nj.gov/treasury/revenue/
32. New Mexico Corporations Division, http://www.sos.state.nm.us/, 505.827.4511 (Phone)/ (505) 827-4387 (Fax)
33. New York Department of State, http://www.dos.ny.gov/, (518) 473-2492 (Phone)/ (518) 474-1418 (Fax)

34. North Carolina Secretary of State, https://www.sosnc.gov/, (919) 814-5400 (Phone)/ (919) 807-2039

35. North Dakota Secretary of State, http://www.nd.gov/sos/, (701) 328-4284 (Phone)/ (701) 328-2992 (Fax)

36. Ohio Secretary of State, http://www.sos.state.oh.us/, (614) 466-3910 (Phone)

37. Oklahoma Secretary of State, https://www.sos.ok.gov/, (405) 521-3912 (Phone)/ (405) 521-3771

38. Oregon Office of the Secretary of State, http://sos.oregon.gov/Pages/default.aspx, (503) 986-2200 (Phone)

39. Pennsylvania Secretary of State, Bureau of Corporations and Charitable Organization, http://www.dos.state.pa.us/portal/server.pt/community/department of state/12405, (717) 787-1057 (Phone)/ (717) 783-2244

40. Rhode Island Secretary of State, http://www.sec.state.ri.us/, (401) 222-3040 (Phone)/ (401) 222-1309

41. South Carolina Secretary of State, https://sdsos.gov/default.aspx, (803) 734-2158 (Phone)/ (803) 734-1614

42. South Dakota Secretary of State, https://sdsos.gov/default.aspx, (605) 773-4845 (Phone)/ (605) 773-4550 (Fax)

43. Tennessee Department of State, http://www.state.tn.us/sos/, (615) 741-2286 (Phone)

44. Texas Secretary of State, http://www.sos.state.tx.us/, (512) 463-5555 (Phone)/ (512) 463-5709 (Fax)

45. Utah Department of Commerce, http://www.utah.gov/government/secretary-of-state.html, (801) 530-4849 (Phone)/ (801) 530-6438

46. Vermont Secretary of State, http://www.sec.state.vt.us/, (802) 828-2386 (Phone)/ (802) 828-2853

47. Virginia State Corporation Commission, http://www.scc.virginia.gov/index.aspx, (804) 371-9733 (Phone)/ (804) 371-9133 (Fax)

48. Washington Secretary of State, https://www.sos.wa.gov/, 360.725.0377 (Phone)/ (360) 664.8781(Fax)

49. West Virginia Secretary of State, http://www.wvsos.com/, (304) 558-8000 (Phone)/ (304) 558.8381(Fax)

50. Wisconsin Department of Financial Institutions, http://www.wdfi.org/, (608) 261-7577 (Phone)/ (608) 267-6813 (Fax)

51. Wyoming Secretary of State, Business Division, http://soswy.state.wy.us/Business/Business.aspx, (307) 777-7311 (Phone)/ (307) 777-5339 (Fax)

STARTING AND LEGITIMIZING YOUR BUSINESS CHECK LIST

STEP ONE: REGISTERING YOUR BUSINESS

____ Registered with domicile state Secretary of State's Office and received Articles of Incorporation forms

____ Registered with IRS and received Employer Identification Number letter

____ Registered with both IRS/domicile state DOR and received sales tax number (if applicable)

STEP TWO: CERTIFICATIONS/TRAINING & LICENSING

____ Researched Industry standards and knows if chosen industry is regulated or unregulated, and what those regulations are.

____ Obtained Industry Specific Certification/Trainings/Licensing

____ Selected a mentor/researching possible mentor candidates

STEP THREE: ON-LINE PRESENCE

____ Website built and launched with Search Engine Optimization (SEO)

____ Researched and created Social Media sites to promote business

____ Created a Mailing List for your business (Email list)

STEP FOUR: BUSINESS INSURANCE

____ Researched Insurance needs and secured Industry specific insurance

____ Developed a working relationship with an Insurance Broker/Agent

____ Secured Workmen's Compensation Insurance (if applicable)

STEP FIVE: CONTRACTUAL AGREEMENT/SERVICE AGREEMENTS

____ Created legal binding Contracts and Service Agreements

____ Created a business relationship with an attorney/legal clinic/legal website to review contracts and service agreements

STEP SIX: HUMAN RESOURCES PRACTICES

____ Type of employee (regular/sub-contractor) researched and selected for business

____ Pre-Employment, Employment and Post-Employment Practices outlined and implemented

____ Sub-Contractor Agreement Completed (if applicable)

____ Human Resources Management Process developed

FIVE STEPS TO ORGANIZING YOUR BUSINESS

1. **Have a DEDICATED and clutter free workspace:** Identify the place you will locate your workspace. Ideally it should be somewhere where there is minimal foot traffic, that inspires creativity and has good lighting. Purchase or repurpose furniture to use in your workspace, and set up your workspace where everything you need is arm's length from your chair. Have all the office supplies you need on hand and put them where they can be easily accessed. When I was raising my children, I taught my children that everything has a place to live and when you get finished using it return it to its home. The same thing applies here; make sure that everything in your workspace has a home to return to once you have finished using it. Put your office supplies in a place where they can be easily accessed, and remember your desk should be off limits to anything that isn't meant to inspire creativity and/or manage your business. Keep this in mind, how your workspace looks affects your mood, creativity and motivation.

   Have your daily to do list in a place where you can review it daily and update it nightly, and keep a calendar on your desk or on the wall next to your desk to write down important dates and appointments. Make a point of looking at your daily to do list and your calendar before you begin working. (This calendar should be separate from your family's calendar.) Utilize the wall space around your desk to keep your workspace free of clutter, and, if possible, mount clear plastic file pockets on your wall to assist you in keeping paperwork off your desk but within reach. Create a system where at the end of each workday or the end of each work session you take a few minutes to process, discard and/or put away everything left out on your desk. It will help you be more productive and creative.

2. **KEEP your personal and your business records separate:** Don't mix business with personal! If your business is a corporation (LLC, S-Corporation, Non-Profit, etc.), it is considered a separate entity, and your finances **MUST** be kept completely separate to maintain the corporate shield that protects your personal assets. Besides reducing legal liability, keeping your business finances separate makes recordkeeping easier, which helps you manager your taxes and business expenses more efficiently. (The IRS website has resources explaining what business and personal records you should keep, how long you should keep them, what forms you need to file, etc.)

   Choose a recordkeeping and accounting system that best fits your business and your personality. Research the banking institutions you are interested in opening an account with. Learn how the bank's merchant account services work and what fees they charge. When choosing an accounting program, learn which accounting software is compatible with the bank's system. Ask if there's a mobile app that will make your business banking easier. Also, research if their business accounts have minimum balance requirement, if they offer 24/7 support or online help and/or if they offer business tax paying services. Keep a complete and separate set of financial, expenses and personal records for you personally and for your business in the accounting software you've chosen. It has even been suggested that you select a business account with a bank other than the one you use to conduct your personal business.

3. **Begin operating your business by getting all the supporting documents and business paraphernalia to market your business:** You never know when opportunity will meet up with preparation and open a door for you to take your business to the next level.

   It is important that you always keep your bottom line in mind at all times. In order to do that you have to be sure you have a good marketing strategy in place to ensure maximum exposure and that you are constantly before your target audience. A huge part of this is branding. Branding is a marketing practice in which a company creates a name, symbol or design that is easily identifiable as belonging to the company. This helps to identify what you sell, and distinguish it from other products and services. It covers everything you do or say as a business – even if your business is just you! Everything that helps a customer or supplier (or anyone) form an impression of your business is your 'brand'. Simply put, your 'brand' is the public face of your business; its personality. And every single element of your business helps to build it – from your voicemail message and social media profile image, to the way you wrap products or how you present yourself when delivering a service. Your brand should be a true representation of who you are as a business, and how you wish to be perceived.

   a. **Logo:** Your logo should be powerful yet easy to remember and recognize. It should make the right impression on your target audience at first glance. It should be on your website, social media profiles, business card, physical business location (if you have one) and on all printed and promotional products.

b. **Business Paraphernalia**: This includes all printed and promotional products that speak to the company's products/services. This includes your business card, letter head, envelopes, etc. that have the ability to speak for your business even when you aren't around.

c. **Online Presence**: It is imperative that you have an online presence. A place where potential clients and interested parties can review your company and secure your products/services. With us being in the computer age not having an online presence is the same as putting money in a pocket with holes in it. This includes your website, social media profiles, and participation in online networking sites within your industry of choice.

d. **Promotional Products:** A strong brand means there is a positive impression of your company among clients/consumers, and that they like doing business with you. Promotional Products include: pens, note pads, mouse pads, pencils, etc. that are stamped with the company's logo.

4. **Develop you 30-second elevator speech** for those impromptu meetings and encounters. Always be ready to market your business. No one is better at selling your business and creating interest than you are!

   An elevator speech is a clear, brief message or "verbal commercial" about your business. It communicates who you are, what services/products your company provides and how they will benefit from what your company has to offer. It's typically about 30 seconds, the time it takes people to ride from the top to the bottom of a building in an elevator. (The idea behind having an elevator speech is that you are prepared to share this information with anyone, at any time, even in an elevator.) It is important to have your speech memorized and practiced. Rehearse your 30 second elevator speech with a friend or in front of a mirror. The important thing is to practice it OUT LOUD. You want it to sound natural. Get comfortable with what you have to say so you can breeze through it when the time comes.

Today your pitch is more apt to take place at a conference or a networking event — or online, where your website and social media pages present your business on your behalf. One way or another, in 20 to 30 seconds or, online, in about 20 words — you need to:

Introduce yourself and your business in a way that seizes interest and makes people want to know more.

- Tell what you do in nontechnical words that someone outside your business or industry can easily understand.
- Describe your product or service and the benefits that it delivers.
- Define the market for your offerings.
- Set yourself apart by highlighting your competitive advantages, your business model, and the people behind your business, such as prominent investors, board members, associations, or business partners.
- Generate interest, prompt questions, and begin to develop a relationship.

5. Develop business relationships with other like-minded business owners and community leaders inside and outside of your chosen Industry

6. One of the most important things you will ever do in life and in business is create business relationships. The connections/relationships will assist you in ways you will never know and that I cannot begin to explain. You may end up with an unexpected mentor, a life-long friend, a source of references and/or business partners. Business owners know other business owners and if they know the products/services you provide they can very easily refer you when the opportunity arises.

7. Cultivate the relationship by making the initial call within 3-5 days from the date you met. Remind them of who you are, your business and how you met. Then share that you would like to find out more about them and what they do. Be genuinely interested in what they have to say, and write it down on a 3x5 card to reference whenever necessary. Set a date and time when you can cat again, and keep that appointment. By keeping contact with them at least twice a month you could be cultivating an invaluable relationship with someone who has the knowledge base you need while navigating through the business atmosphere today!

www.ingramcontent.com/pod-product-compliance
Lightning Source LLC
Chambersburg PA
CBHW032017190326
41520CB00007B/511
9787815323531